Mrs Heginbottom

Contents

Author
Aidan Warlow
Contributors
Chris Buckton
Gloria Campbell
Ruth Crow
Louis Fidge
Heather Hanrott
John Harris
Chris McIllroy
Nick Pepin
Anne Reyersbach
Jane Salt

What I am Really Like

Have you got a new teacher this term? If so, you can tell him or her what you are really like.

1 Write the title Things I can do. Then you can begin I am quite good at _____ or I can _____. These questions may give you ideas:

What games can you play? Which are you good at?

Can you swim? If so, which strokes and how far?

Can you cook? If so, what can you cook?

Can you draw? If so, what are you best at drawing?

What else can you do? Can you skip, ride a bike, jump down five steps at a time, look after an animal, sing?

2 Write the title Things I would like. Then you can start like this:

If I could be any famous real person, I would like to be _____. (Say why. What would you do?)

If I could be a character from a book or a television programme I would like to be _____.

If I could do anything I like in the world tomorrow, I would _____. (Think of something really exciting.)

3 Write the title My Favourite Things. **Then you can start like this:**

The best story book I have ever read is _____. The main character in it is _____. (Write another sentence saying what sort of things he or she does.)

The television programme that I most enjoy is _____. (What are the best things in it?)

The best game I ever play is _____. (Tell us why you enjoy it.)

What I like most about school is _____.

What else do you like at home or school or out of doors?

Facts and opinions

Now look over all that you have written. **Pick out four facts** – things that are definitely true and that nobody will argue about. For example, if you can stand on your head and sometimes do so, that is a fact.

Write **F** next to the four facts.

Pick out four opinions – things that you think, but that others might not agree with. For example, you might think 'Match of the Day' is the best programme on television but other people might prefer something else.

Write **O** next to the four opinions.

3

Roald Dahl at Work

Primary school children often vote for Roald Dahl as their favourite author. Would that be true in your school?

We went to interview him in the old summer house in his garden where he does his writing.

What gives you ideas for stories?

Roald Dahl   I suddenly get an idea for a plot and write it down quickly before I forget it. Then I work on it. The story *grows* at the desk while you write. You never know where it is going to.

What's your advice to children when they write stories?

Roald Dahl   Never be satisfied with what you write! Don't immediately think you've written a good story. Be self-critical. Make it better! Don't be depressed if you don't write a good story first time.

Do you make rough drafts?

Roald Dahl   I write a complete first page. Then I say "It's not funny enough!" or "It's not exciting enough!" and I rewrite it about ten times. It's a mass of crossings out. Of course you haven't got time to do that in the classroom. But you may often have to cross things out to make them better.

A page of Roald Dahl's handwritten manuscript, with many crossings-out and corrections.

A page from Roald Dahl's
Charlie and the Great Glass Elevator.

---

proceeded to tie a knot with its two ends, a good strong knot, left over right, then right over left. When it had pulled the knot tight, there remained about five yards of one end hanging loose. This was the end with the eyes on it. But it didn't hang loose for long. It quickly curled itself into the shape of a huge hook and the hook stuck straight out sideways from the Elevator as though waiting for something else to hook itself on to it.

While all this was going on, nobody had noticed what the other Knids were up to. 'Mr Wonka!' Charlie cried. 'Look at the others! What *are* they doing?'

What indeed?

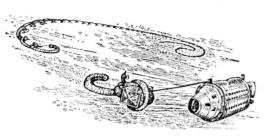

These, too, had all changed shape and had become longer, but not nearly so long or so thin as the first one. Each of them had turned itself into a kind of thick rod and the rod was curled around at both ends – at the tail-end and at the head end – so that it made a double-ended hook. And now all the hooks were linking up into one long chain . . . one thousand Knids . . . all joining together and curving around in the sky to make a chain of Knids half a mile long or more! And the Knid at the very front of the chain (whose front hook was not, of course, hooked up to anything) was leading them in a wide circle and sweeping in toward the Great Glass Elevator.

73

A page from the finished book.

What sort of stories do **you** like to write most? Funny or serious? True-to-life or make-believe?

What helps you to start a story?

   ideas from the teacher?
   ideas from pictures?
   ideas of your own?
   a mixture of all these?

Do you agree with Roald Dahl about crossing out?

How could your own stories be improved – apart from spelling and handwriting?

Turn to the next page for some ideas for writing.

As Roald Dahl says, you haven't always got time to make as many rough copies as he does. But you should:

1 Check over everything you write; correct and improve it.

2 Always make rough copies for poems.

Ideas for Stories

Choose which story you want to write. Then start your story on the left. Follow one black arrow to continue. Then follow one blue arrow. Carry on with the story adding your own ideas.

She asked me to help her...
(Where did you get them from? What happened?)

she wanted to collect _____
(old engines? old magic books? unwanted pets? or something else?)

She didn't want anyone else to know...
(Why? Where did she keep them? Was she found out?)

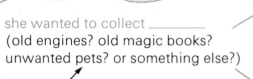

My gran was always thinking of new things to do. One day she announced that _____

She ran out of fuel and had to parachute out...
(Where did she land? What happened?)

she would learn to fly an aeroplane...
(Who taught her? Was she a good pupil?)

She got mixed up with a gang of smugglers...
(How did she meet them? What happened?)

(Or did something else happen?)

(Can you think of a different surprising thing she might have done?)

I kept a watch on what she (or he) did . . .
(Was she running away from something? Why? What happened?)

In it lived a very unusual girl (or boy) . . .
(What was unusual about her? What was her name? Describe her. Did you talk to her?)

She kept some very odd pets . . .
(Describe them. Was one very dangerous?)

(Did something else happen?)

In the corner of a lonely field stood a yellow caravan . . .

Looking through drawers I came across an old diary . . .
(Did it have something mysterious in it?)

Nobody ever used it so I thought I would borrow it . . .
(Why? What was it like inside? Were you nervous?)

I borrowed a horse and went off on the most exciting holiday of my life . . .

(Or did the owner come back and catch you? Or did something else happen?)

(Can you think of a different story about it?)

Titles

A title should sound interesting and tell your reader something about the story.

It could be somebody's name: *Worzel Gummidge, Black Beauty, Fantastic Mr Fox*.

Or it could be about what happens: *Lion at Large, Murder in the Woodshed, Mountain Rescue*.

Look through a shelf of library books to see what other authors do.

My Private Zoo

Imagine that you are going to start your own zoo. You have been given plenty of money and some land to put it on. You must plan it very carefully.

 In rough, make a list of the animals, insects and birds you would like to keep in your zoo.

Decide on **one** interesting creature and work out how to keep it happy and comfortable. Don't just put it into a cage! You must **research** into how it lived in the wild and then find ways of making its life in the zoo not too different. For example, monkeys need trees to swing on and a hippopotamus needs a muddy pool.

Library research

Look up your creature in an animal book or encyclopaedia. Write the answers to these questions as rough notes.

1 What countries does it live in? Is it hot or cold there?

2 What sort of home does it live in?

3 What does it eat?

4 Does it have any enemies?

5 Is there anything else specially interesting about it?

Now copy out and fill in this chart using your notes.

The life of a _____ (Name of creature)

In the wild

It lives in _____ (which countries?)

where it is _____ (hot? cold? what else?)

It makes its home in _____ (trees? holes? where?)

It eats _____.

Its enemies are _____.

(Add any other interesting facts about it)

In captivity

In this country it would need to be kept _____ (warm? cool? what?)

We could keep it in _____.

We could feed it on _____.

For exercise it would need _____.

The main difference between its life in the wild and in captivity would be _____.

Now draw a careful picture of the place where you are going to keep your animal. It might be a field or a house or a cage, with everything needed to make it happy and comfortable. Show everything clearly.

Making Rough Notes

You make rough notes to help you remember things.

You do not have to use good handwriting, as long as you can read them.

You can cross out and alter words.

You do not need to write in complete sentences.

Extra Ideas

1 Think what would happen if your creature escaped. Would it manage to live on its own? Where would it sleep? What would it eat? What would people say and do if they saw it? Write a story about what happened.

2 Do you think it is cruel to keep any wild animals in captivity? Explain why.

Ideas from my Paintbox

Uncle John's Paintbox

One day
  He came to say,
Would you like to see,
  My paintbox.

Black is a burglar running into the
  night,
A hidden lucky cat;
Or coal about to light,
The hidden mysteries in your mind.

Brown appears as trees bowing in an
  Autumn wind,
Or newly made hot buttered toast,
Melting chocolate by the fire,
An escaping fox.

Green is the harvest fields,
Or new spring grass.
Dense African jungle
Or a parrot's tail.

Blue might be a pool, deep and cool,
Or the cold around your feet.
The sea, angry and restless,
Or a clear sky on a summer day.

Red could be blood oozing out of a cut,
Flames dancing in the fire,
Or a juicy apple about to fall,
The scene after the Glencoe massacre.

Silver could be tears streaming the
  face,
Dew in the morning grass,
Or hail hitting the fragile window pane,
A crown upon a prince's head.

Gold is the harvest moon, sun of night,
Treasure deep below,
Or coins gleaming in the golden light,
Ripe wheat shivering in the cold wind.

Yellow is the street lights at night,
Or a flickering candle light,
Bananas hanging high above,
Lion's teeth glistening in the sunlight.

White might be a tiger's whiskers,
Ashes of a dying fire,
Ghosts on a nightly haunt,
Or rooftops in winter.

Kevin O'Dowda (11)

Are there any lines in this poem that you think are specially good? Pick out the two lines that you like best. Are there any you don't like very much?

Write your own poem in the same way. Make a rough copy first so that you can add ideas later or change words. You can start Black is _____ and work through as many colours as you like.

Extra Idea

Think about different sorts of weather. What happens when it rains, when it is windy, when it is sunny, when it snows? Write a poem describing the things that you have noticed. One verse can begin Windy days are . . . . Other verses can begin Snow is . . . Sunshine is . . . Rain is . . . Thunder is . . . .

Pirates

Look at this picture of pirates. The captain is watching over his men as they bury treasure.

 Write the title Pirates. Then **write a description** of what is happening in this picture. What sounds can you hear? What can you see? Mention all the things that make it seem creepy. You can begin The full moon shone brightly over the sea _____

This description can be the beginning of your story. Look at the next page to see how it carries on.

 This is the same scene twenty years later. In the cave are three skulls beside the treasure. Whose skulls are they? What do you think happened? Why is the treasure still lying there?

Carry on with your story of what happened on that moonlit night.

Extra Idea

Look up 'Pirates' in a library book or encyclopaedia. Make rough notes to answer these questions:

Were there any women pirates?

What were the names of some famous pirates? What did they do?

Whose treasure did they steal? Where did they operate?

How long ago did they live?

You can then write about them and make a wall display called 'Pirates' with plenty of your own pictures.

Good and Bad Days

Do you enjoy some school days more than others?

What are the things that make a school day good? Is it the teacher being nice to you or making a new friend or going out somewhere?

What makes a day seem a bad day? Is it somebody being horrid, or having to do some boring work or getting into trouble?

Think of a recent **good** day. Make some rough notes to remind you of:

how the day started;
all the good things that happened;
who you were with and what they said;
how the day ended.

Now write the title A Good Day in My Life. Write about the day, including plenty of details so that somebody who wasn't there can imagine just what it was like.

Extra Ideas

1 Write about a **bad** day. Call it A Bad Day in My Life.

2 Keep a regular diary. Use an ordinary notebook, not a printed diary, so that you will have space for special long entries and pictures.

Which Pet?

Pet (average life-span)	Items that need to be paid for	Types of food	Can you stroke it?	Can you play with it?	Jobs to be done
Rabbit (5 years)	Large wood and wire hutch. Sawdust or shavings, straw or hay. Water bottle, food dish.	Dry rabbit food. Root vegetables, grass and dandelion leaves. Water.	Sometimes	No	Feed and water. Clean hutch regularly.
Cat (up to 14 years)	Basket or box bed with blanket or cushion. Food, water and milk dishes. Litter tray. Vaccinations.	Tinned cat meat, fresh meat, fish. Milk, water.	Yes	When young	Feed. Change water daily. Clean litter tray. House train. Treat for fleas and worms as necessary.
Gerbil (3 years)	Metal and plastic cage. Shavings or sawdust. Food dish, water bottle.	Dry seed food. Small amounts of green vegetables or carrots. Water.	Yes	No	Feed and water. Clean cage daily.
Woodlice	Box with lid and breathing holes (no cost).	Damp, rotting wood and leaves.	No	No	Sprinkle with water every day. Keep in a cool place. Watch them eat, draw them. Don't keep longer than five days.
Dog (up to 14 years)	Basket and rug. Collar and lead. License. Toys. Food and water dishes. Vaccinations.	Tinned dog meat, fresh meat, biscuits. Large raw bones. Water.	Yes	Yes	Feed. Change water daily. Exercise daily. House train. Train to be obedient and undestructive. Bath and groom regularly. Treat for worms as necessary.
Hamster (2–3 years)	Large metal and plastic cage with sleeping section. Food dish. Sawdust or shavings. Exercise wheel, toys.	Dry seed food. Cereals, fruit, nuts, vegetables, green plants. Water. Enjoys gnawing wood.	Yes	No	Feed in the evening. Change water daily. Clean cage daily.

Study this chart. Which do you think is the best pet for someone of your age? Why do you think that?

Which do you think is the worst pet? Why do you think so?

Write the title The Best Pet and explain which of these pets you would choose. Describe the disadvantages as well as the advantages.

Or think of another pet which is not on the chart. First write down what the chart would have said about its home, food, etc. Then explain why you think it would be a good pet.

Look at the Evidence

This photograph was taken in 1906 in London. All the children had to dress in their best Sunday clothes for the photograph. It is clear **evidence** of what schools were like then.

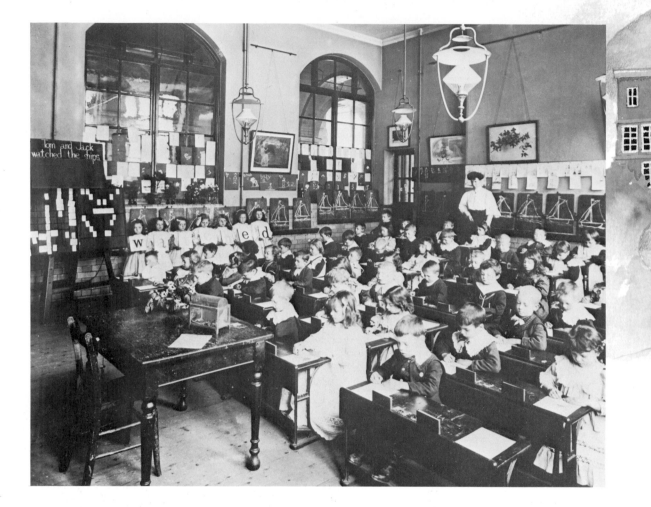

Look at the photograph carefully. **In rough**, write a list of eight things that make it different from your own modern classroom. For example, what do you notice about the front boy's feet? How are the boys and girls seated? Why? How many are there? Does the teacher look strict?

Now write the title A School in 1906

What do you think life was like at this school? **Describe it** for somebody who has not seen this picture. You can start In 1906 school children had to _____ Use the ideas in your rough list to help you.

Would you have liked going to that school? Explain why.

16

My School

Imagine that you have to describe your school to a child living in 1906.

Begin by making rough notes to answer these questions. You may have to do some research or ask people to help you.

Is your school old or modern? How old is it?

What is it built of?

How many children are there in your class?

How do children sit and work?

What do you have in your school that was not invented in 1906?

What are the best things you do?

How do the teachers treat you?

What are you allowed to do which a 1906 child was probably not allowed to do?

What do you wear?

Now write a full description, using your rough notes to help you. Add any details that will make it interesting, so that the 1906 child can really imagine your school.

Commas

When you list three or more things in a sentence, you separate them with a comma so they don't get muddled up.

We have three rabbits, two stick insects, four gerbils and a fat toad.

My friends are Maribel, Lee, Jake, Chris and Leila.

There is no comma between the last two things because the word **and** separates them.

Litter

Open your eyes and look around. You will see litter almost everywhere polluting our environment. Some children in Luton were fed up with seeing all the litter around their school so they decided to do something about it.

They launched a 'Campaign in Luton Against Pollution' (CLAP for short!) and they thought of a catchy slogan:

PICKA BITTA LITTA UP FIND A BIN TO PUT IT IN

Think of all the different sorts of litter you might find near your school. Why do you think people leave litter? Why do you think it is a bad thing?

What do you do with *your* sweet wrappings when you are out of doors?

Now plan your own campaign week. How are you going to persuade people not to spread litter?

Here are some ideas:

Think up some really catchy slogans. They could be funny like the Luton children's one, or more forceful like *Don't be a litter lout!*

Give your campaign a name like Class 3 Against Pollution (CAP).

Design a badge. First make a rough copy. Draw a circle on a piece of card and copy out your design. Cut it out and fix it on your chest with a ring of sellotape.

Design some really eye-catching posters pointing out the bad things about litter from your list. Think about where you should pin them up.

Ask your Head whether you can tell the rest of the school about your campaign in Assembly.

Do you have any more ideas?

Double Monsters

There are many stories of strange monsters who were a mixture of two different creatures. Here are a couple of examples:

This savage monster was called the Minotaur. From the neck downwards it was a barrel-chested, two-metre high human being. From the neck upwards it was a shaggy bull. Its eyes flashed fire; it had razor fangs and it fed on human flesh.

Griffins were huge, fierce creatures. Each had the body of a lion and the wings and head of an eagle. They were sometimes called the 'hounds of Zeus'. Shunning sunlight, it was their job to guard gold mines and hidden treasure through the hours of darkness.

 Now you invent another double monster, a mixture of two creatures. Draw a picture of it and give it a name.

Write a story about the terrible things it does. You must describe the monster very carefully in your story and explain how somebody tries to catch it.

Apostrophe s

Remember   Use **'s** when something belongs to somebody

The minotaur's breath
Sadia's hair
Joe's pet mouse

Extra Idea

Use books from the library to find out about these creatures:
the Phoenix, the Cyclops, the Sphinx, Grendel.

When I was Little

What can you remember about when you were little? Do you remember your first toys? What were they?

your first teacher? What did you do in her class?

your first friends? What were they like? What did you do together?

any special things that happened?

Have your parents ever told you about the funny things you did or said?

In rough, make a list of all the things you can remember.

Now write the title When I was Little. Write about yourself using your list to help you. You might like to start The first thing I can remember _____.

Draw a picture of yourself when you were little.

Special People

A girl called Rachel wrote this poem about her mother.

She tried very hard to think of things that made her *different* from other mothers.

My Mum

Always making rude remarks about herself.
Never gives herself a compliment.
Has brown shadows under her eyes,
Thick eyes like chocolate.
Freckles are scattered around her face
And up her arms.
She has red curls
That touch her shoulders
And bounce when she walks.
She has a big generous smile.
She likes eating
But restricts herself to salad.
She has a quick brisk walk,
Only runs when forced.

This is how she wrote it.

1 In rough she made a list of all the things that made her mother special. It looked untidy but it gave her lots of ideas for her poem.

quite tall
red hair
freckles
nice smile
eats alot
walks fast
makes a rude comment about herself
thick eyes.

2 She rewrote it, describing each thing as clearly as she could. Some lines were a bit long. She split them into two to make them look more like a poem.

Always making rude ~~comments~~ remarks about herself
Never gives herself a compliment.
She has brown ~~shoulders~~ shadows under her eyes
and thick eyes like chocolate.
She has freckles are scattered around her face and
up her arms
She has red curles of hair ~~here~~ that touch her
shoulders
~~which~~ and bounce when she walks.
She has a nice big generous smile.
She likes eating. but only salad
She has a quick brisk walk and
only runs when forced ~~to~~.

3 Then she made a final beautiful copy with a picture.

Then a boy called Frank Easton made this rough copy of a poem about his friend.

> ~~walking along~~
>   nut
> thinks hes tough ~~boy~~
> wears Doc martins
> blue and white sweat band
> ~~lots of~~ with ginger hair
> freckles
>   ice
> tries to look cool
> likes wispa bars
> ~~he leans against the wall~~
> calls people names
> ~~does not really mean it~~
> ‿ he starts laughing
> you now he does not mean it

This was his final version.

Portrait of a Friend

> He thinks he's a tough nut
> In his Doc Martin boots
> And his blue and white sweat band.
> You'd notice him anywhere
> With his ginger hair
> And freckles.
> He leans against the wall
> Trying to look ice cool
> Taking bites from his Wispa bar
> And calling people names.
> But then he starts laughing
> And you know he doesn't mean it.

Can you see how Frank changed his rough copy until it was exactly what he wanted?

Now write a poem about someone **you** know very well. Begin, as Rachel and Frank did, with a **list** of all the things that make the person special.

Cross out anything you don't like. Change or add words to make it better. Check the spellings.

Copy it out in your best handwriting. You can also draw a picture of the person.

In the Dark

Have you ever lain awake at night and looked at the shapes in the dark? Everything looks different. Ordinary shapes, like the lampshade or chest of drawers, cast shadows and you think they are weird creatures or spooks.

In the Dark

A man runs across the ceiling
Of my bedroom,
Someone with long hands patterned with leaves.

The wardrobe looks like a huge bird,
Six times bigger than an eagle.
I don't like the dark.

The flowers on the table near the window
Catch the street light as it shines on them
Then they look like little heads.

When the wind blows it comes through the door,
And to me it sounds like a ghost
Worming its way through the cracks.
At night everything looks different
All sorts of ghostly shapes
In the dark.

Jane Pridmore

This poem is written by another child who is scared in the dark.

But this child happily listens to the sounds of his family downstairs.

Shadows in my Mind

The glow of the dim oil lamp flickers.
I see shadows in my mind
   lurking about beyond the lamp.
Dark shadows that move in the light
I see them getting nearer and nearer.
I stand, my heart thumping, my eyes
   water.
A cold shiver goes down my back.
But I'm only thinking of thoughts in
   my mind.

Hilary (9)

Bedtime

All safe in bed
Ready to say goodnight to my mother
I haven't anything to do but just go to
   sleep
I can hear my mother and father's
   voices
The television, a car starting outside
I like to go to sleep because it is silent
But another day comes
To get working again.

Errol (10)

Now you write a poem about lying awake at night. You might be frightened or you might be relaxed.

You can begin by making a rough copy. Write down all the ideas you have – what you can see and hear and think and imagine. Then write out a neat copy with a picture.

Rhyming

Your poems will probably be much better if they don't rhyme. It is very difficult to find words which rhyme and which also have the right meaning.

Jake

Read this story about a small boy called Jake. Do you think there is anything unusual about him?

One morning when Jake was five he had lain for a while listening to bird sounds and traffic sounds and decided that it would be a good hour before anyone else was up, so he'd slipped downstairs to the kitchen for a cup of milk.

He'd taken his mug off its special hook and was opening the fridge when he'd realized that there was someone else in the room. Not Mum – she'd have started talking. Not Dad – there'd have been cigarette smoke. His brother Martin never got up till he had to. No, there was a stranger sitting by the table, watching him.

Jake turned with the bottle in his hand and said, "Who are you? What are you doing in our house?"

"You're Jake," said a quiet, slow voice.

"Who are you?" said Jake.

"I'm your grandfather."

"No you aren't. Granpa's across the sea."

"They made me come home. They didn't give me time to write to your Mum."

Jake felt for the mug he'd left on top of the fridge, poured it two-thirds full of milk and put the bottle back. He could feel Granpa watching him all the time. He was proud of the way he did things for himself – several of his sighted friends weren't allowed to pour their own milk because their Mums thought they'd spill – so he didn't mind showing off to Granpa.

"Shall I tell you a story about crocodiles?" asked Granpa suddenly.

"A true story?"

"I don't make things up, Jake."

When Jake came down again the kitchen was empty. He found his milk and went to the lounge. It smelt of bedrooms, as if somebody had been sleeping on the sofa, but Granpa was standing over by the window, watching him again.

"You can sit down," said Jake. "But you mustn't put your feet on the chairs."

"I thought you couldn't see anything at all, Jake."

"Course I can't. And I won't ever, either. I don't mind."

"How did you know I was here?"

"I just knew."

Peter Dickinson

At what point in the story did you realise Jake was blind? How did you guess?

Think about how Jake finds his way around and knows where things are. If you blindfolded yourself, would you manage as well as he does?

What do you think Jake's life is like?

Blind people become very clever at finding their way about – with the help of a guide dog.

They can also cook, make and mend things, and write with a typewriter. They learn to become lawyers, teachers, musicians, carvers of wood and stone, piano tuners . . . can you think of other jobs they might do?

They can also read by using special writing called **Braille**. It consists of little bumps on the page which they can feel as they run their hands over it.

Braille Alphabet

A	B	C	D	E	F	G	H	I	J

K	L	M	N	O	P	Q	R	S	T

U	V	W	X	Y	Z	and	for	of	the

Imagine that you were blind, but still living at your present home. Describe part of a day in your life. You can begin I woke up one morning and could hear the sounds of _____. Describe how you managed to do everything.

Shape Poems

Shape poems describe something interesting in words and in shape.

Look at these two poems.

Nazan (9)

ICE CREAM
You lick viciously and very quickly. It starts to melt. It's dripping! Catch it! Trickles down tongue. Gorgeous!

Leaves whoossh as the leaves flutter down down to the ground like a bird. as the Sun peers up at the leaves and goes back to its sleep.

Rubina Rehrman (9)

Do the words describe leaves and eating ice cream well?

Can you think of another good sentence to describe each of these exactly?

Leaves falling off the trees.
How ice cream feels in your mouth.

Now you write a shape poem. This is how you do it.

Choose something to describe. It could be:

a football   or a snake   or a tree   or a snail

Then, **in rough**, write an interesting sentence about it. Include words that really describe how it looks or moves or what it reminds you of.

Draw the shape and copy the words in so that they fit.

Here are some more shape poems to look at.

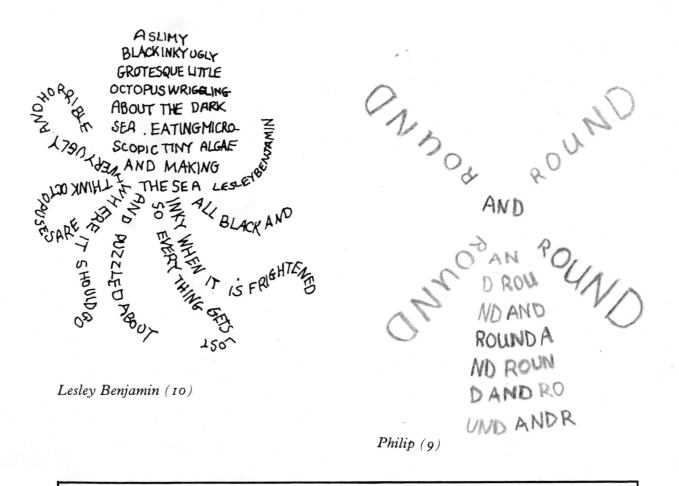

Lesley Benjamin (10)

Philip (9)

Extra Idea

Perhaps your shape poems can be cut out and pasted onto a large sheet to make a collage picture.

What Does it Remind You of?

Read this poem. Do you think that David describes the alligator clearly?

Its mouth is like a cave,
Its back is like some burnt toast.
It can move in the water like a snake on land
And it rips its prey apart
Like a machine digging into the earth.
Its skin is like the bricks on a house.

David Streak (9)

Can you think of any other things that the alligator's mouth or back or skin remind you of?

Look at this photograph of a Greater Horseshoe Bat. Why do you think it is called that?

In rough, write down what it reminds you of like this:

Its face is like a _____.
Its ears are like _____.
Its wings are like _____.

What else do you notice about it? What would you think if you saw it flying around?

From your rough notes, write a poem called The Bat.

Look at these pictures. What do they remind you of?

 Choose one of these, or find something of your own to describe.
Write a poem about it, saying what it reminds you of.

What was the Matter with You?

Have you ever been off school because you were unwell? What was the matter with you? What was it like? How did you feel?

Was it horrid all the time – or was there anything about it you enjoyed?

Describe a time when you were ill or hurt. Tell us how it started, what people said, how you felt and what happened afterwards.

A Class Survey

Ask round the class to find out how many people have had some sort of illness or any accidents. You can **make a graph** like one of these:

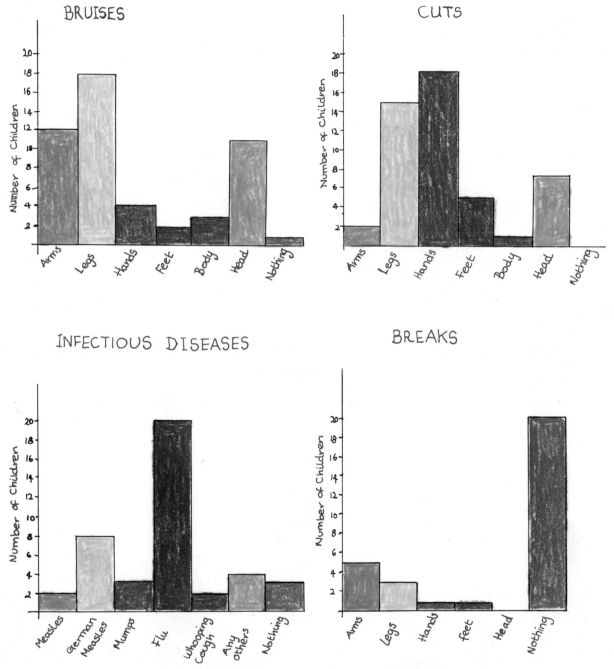

Then answer these questions:

Which parts of the body most often get injured? What sort of injuries are most common? Why do you think that is? Which are least common? What sorts of illnesses are most common? Which are least common?

Who in your class has had the fewest things wrong with him or her?

The Words People Say

In comics we put bubbles around the words people say like this:

In stories we put **speech marks** around the words people say like this:

"Look at this Dad! Quick!" shouted Moira.
"What is it?" asked her dad.
Moira showed him her strange contraption. "It's the first ever helicopter powered by fizzy lemonade," she said proudly.
"How does it work?" he asked.
Moira explained, "You shake the fuel tank hard like this... switch on the engine and..."
There was a loud explosion and Dad got soaked.

Speech marks are like comic bubbles. They go round people's words.

We put " when people start to speak.
We put " after the last word they say.

Now read this comic strip.

 Decide on names for the characters. Then **write it out as a story**, using speech marks instead of bubbles.

You can begin: (name) and (name) crept up to the castle. The moon shone on its massive walls.

"Look," whispered (name). "There's a light in that tower."

Carry on with the story. Does the rescue plan work or does it run into unexpected problems?

Think of a title.

Ideas from Other Authors

These plots are all from books that you can probably find in a library. Choose one to write a story about.

You can change the characters' names and alter anything else you like. Later, you can read the book and compare it with your version.

Lion at Large by Richard Parker

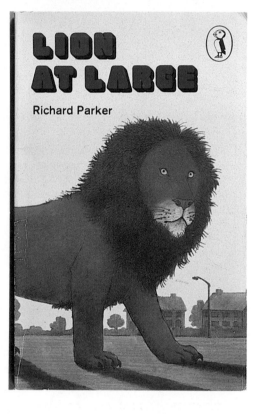

"Mum, listen," said Barry. "I saw a lion out of the window last night. Just wandering about in the road it was. Then it went right down through the orchard."

But of course Barry's mum doesn't believe him. Nor does anyone else. Then a girl in his class called Ingrid says she heard a lion's roar.

Why do you think the lion was there?
What would Ingrid and Barry have done?

Write your own version of the story.

Conversation

Conversation helps to make a story interesting.

It can tell us what a character is thinking:
"I wish I was safely back at home," said Eric.

It can tell us what is happening:
"Look out! The ceiling's collapsing!" shouted Emily.

It can tell us how people talk to each other:
"Hi, Roger! Do you want to come out with us after school?" said Jan.

Remember to include plenty of conversation in your stories. And remember speech marks (" ").

No More School by William Mayne

The village school teacher has gone off sick and the school has to close.

After a while the children get bored and wish school would start again. One of them has a great idea – they can run it themselves without any teachers!

Think how **you** would run your school if your teachers were all away. Write a story about it.

George's Marvellous Medicine by Roald Dahl

Most grandmothers are nice and kind. But George's was horrible – always grousing, grouching, grumbling and griping.

One day George concocts an amazing magic medicine for her – hair shampoo, floor polish, curry powder, everything he can find – and cooks it up into a frothy brew.

The effect on his Grandma is amazing!

What do you think happened to Granny? Write your version of the story.

Extra Idea

Look through a shelf of fiction in the library. The front covers and titles may give you good ideas for stories.

Helping Other People to Choose Books

Book reviews tell you two things: what the book is about and whether the writer thinks other people would like it. Read this review by a girl called Miriam.

Charlotte's Web by E. B. Wright

The best book I have ever read is Charlotte's Web. It is very imaginative and always exciting.

The part I like best is where Wilbur the pig escapes and all the farm animals are cheering him along. But the tired little pig ends up in the barn again.

The tale is not always happy. Almost at the end, the pig's best friend Charlotte, a spider, dies. At this stage I could hardly read for tears but when I finished I was happy again for Charlotte had left sons and daughters.

Boys and girls over the age of seven will like this book and so will grown ups. I have read it at least three times.

 Does Miriam's review make you want to read the book? If you have read Charlotte's Web, do you agree with Miriam's review?

 Choose a story that you have read or listened to and **write a review** of it. It should contain the answers to these questions:

How much did you like the book? Why?

Who is the best character in it? Tell us one very interesting thing that he or she does.

Perhaps you can make a display of your reviews in the library so that other people can decide what to read next.

Fan Mail

Authors like to receive letters from children who have enjoyed their books. Here is a letter that Sean Berrick wrote to Helen Cresswell.

14 Rushton Street,
Nottingham,
NO14 F1O.
26 April

Dear Mrs Cresswell,

I am writing to tell you how much we are enjoying reading your book The Secret World of Polly Flint in our class. My favourite character is Aunt Em because she is always nagging at Polly and she is very tidy. We have got to the part where Polly meets the baby.

Our teacher took us to Rufford Park where you story takes place We saw the lake and the animal graves but not the tunnel. Did you make that bit up?

Do you like football? We watched Wales beat Spain 3-0 last night on television and my favourite Liverpool player Rush scored two goals. Mum kept coming in to tell us to stop shouting.

I want to read a lot more of your books.

With love from

Sean Berrick

date and address

Dear Mr or **Mrs** or **Miss . . .**

what he most liked about the book

some news about himself

ends **Love from**. You can end **Yours sincerely** if you want to be less friendly

 You can **write a letter** to one of these:

an author
a sports personality
a television personality

Explain why you admire his or her work. Say something interesting about yourself.

Punctuating a Letter

capital letters for the month, places, people	89 Raven Street,	comma
	Cranbury,	comma
	Dorset.	full stop
	DT12 9SP	
	13th May, 1986	

comma   Dear Mr Garfield,

A Fantastic Trick

Read this story by a Russian writer called Maxim Gorky.

When the Wolves Came Down

One year there was a severe frost and the wolves started coming down from the fields, right into the yard. Sometimes they devoured one of the dogs, or frightened a horse or ate a drunken watchman. They made a lot of trouble.

Father would take his rifle, put his snow shoes on, and go out to the fields and bring back a wolf or two. He would skin them, stuff the heads and put glass eyes in, which he was very clever at.

One night Uncle Mikhail went out to the lavatory and suddenly came running back, his hair on end, his eyes popping out, and too paralysed to say anything. His trousers were falling down and he got tangled up in them and tripped over. 'A wolf!'' he whispered.

Everyone seized the first thing they could lay their hands on and rushed out to the lavatory with lighted torches. And sure enough there was a wolf poking its head out from the seat. They fired at it, beat it, but this didn't have the slightest effect.

Then they took a closer look, and found a skin and an empty head, with the front legs nailed to the seat!

How do you think Uncle Mikhail felt? What do you think he said? Do you think it was a good trick?

Write a story called The Fantastic Trick. Tell how you or someone else played a really clever trick on some friends and scared them.

Describe carefully
   when and where the trick was played,
   how it was carried out,
   what people said.

Try to make it seem true with people behaving as they really would in real life.

Rules

Look at this picture carefully.

Make a list of eight things that people are doing wrong. For example: The boys are playing football in the road.

Write the title Rules. Make a list of rules to stop people doing the wrong things. Say why they are wrong. For example: You must not park your car on yellow lines because the road gets too crowded. This can cause traffic jams.

You can begin each rule You must not _____ because _____. Don't just say 'because it is dangerous'. Explain why it is dangerous.

Is it Fair?

MUSEUM

NO PERSON UNDER 14 ALLOWED IN UNLESS WITH AN ADULT.
~MUSEUM CURATOR~

·PARK·

NO BALLGAMES
NO PICNICS
NO BICYCLES
ALL DOGS ON LEADS

PARK SUPERINTENDANT

FLATS

NO PLAYING ON THE STAIRS.
NO PETS.
NO LOUD MUSIC

LANDLORD

In this picture, some of the rules might seem wrong or unfair to children. What do you think?

Look at each rule in turn and think why it was made. What would happen if there wasn't a rule?

A girl called Kate wrote this letter to her landlord:

26th October 1986

Flat 18,
Ibstock Mansions,
Whitby Street,
Wrexham,
LL3 9RF

Dear Sir,

I am writing to complain about the rule banning loud music in our flats.

I love music. I have over fifty records and all my friends come in to listen to them. If we didn't listen to records in the evening, we would be playing outside and causing trouble.

My sister is learning the trumpet at school. She hopes to be a professional. Our flat is the only place where she can practise.

I know that the walls are thin and people might get disturbed. I suggest that extra thick felting be fitted round the walls and floors to prevent the noise spreading.

Yours faithfully,

Kate Rickaby

Note that Kate writes:

her address and the date

Dear Sir because Kate doesn't know the man's name

clear reasons why she is complaining

a sensible suggestion for solving the problem

Yours faithfully at the end because she does not know the man.

 Do you think Kate's letter would change the landlord's mind?

Now you pick out a rule from the picture which you don't agree with. **Write a polite letter** to the person in charge explaining why the rule should be changed.

Extra Idea

Think of a rule that you have to obey which you think should be changed.

Write a polite letter to the person who made the rule asking for it to be changed.

Ideas for Cheap Presents

 People always enjoy presents that you have made yourself. Here are some instructions for things to make at home. Perhaps you have suggestions for improving them.

A tin can telephone for a child

You will need

2 tin cans or plastic pots

A piece of string about 10 metres long

What to do

1 Make a very small hole in the middle of the base of each can or pot. (You can use a hammer and nail, or an old fashioned tin opener. Ask an adult to help you.)

2 Thread one end of the string through the holes in each pot and knot the end. The knot is on the inside of the pot.

Do the same with the other end of the string and the second pot.

3 Hold your telephone so that the string is stretched tight and doesn't touch anything.

The string really does carry the sound!

A feast for the birds in winter

You will need

Pieces of food, such as stale crusts, lumps of vegetable and apple and cornflakes rolled in peanut butter

A piece of string about 50 cm long

What to do

1 Tie a knot in one end of the piece of string

Thread the pieces of food on to the string.

2 Hang it on a tree or washing line.

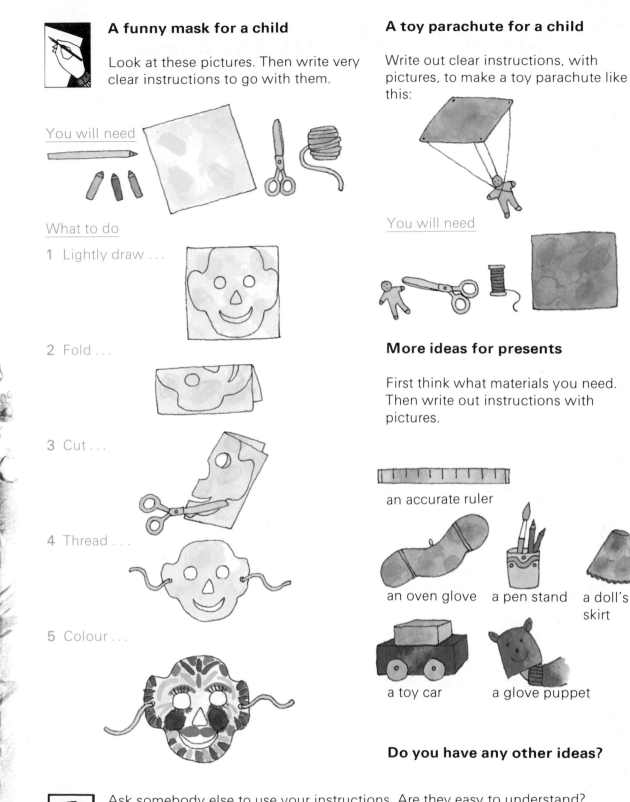

A funny mask for a child

Look at these pictures. Then write very clear instructions to go with them.

You will need

What to do

1 Lightly draw . . .

2 Fold . . .

3 Cut . . .

4 Thread . . .

5 Colour . . .

A toy parachute for a child

Write out clear instructions, with pictures, to make a toy parachute like this:

You will need

More ideas for presents

First think what materials you need. Then write out instructions with pictures.

an accurate ruler

an oven glove   a pen stand   a doll's skirt

a toy car   a glove puppet

Do you have any other ideas?

Ask somebody else to use your instructions. Are they easy to understand? Did you miss anything out?

What are You Going to Write?

Look at the picture on the left and think what might have happened. Then decide on one of these ways of writing about it.

A story Imagine you and a friend landed on this island. How did you get there? Perhaps you were wrecked and need rescuing? Or did you go there to explore? What happened?

A poem Imagine the beautiful or dangerous or unusual things on the island. Make a rough list of ideas and turn it into a poem.

Or write a poem about how it feels to be stranded in a strange place a long way from home.

Instructions Explain how to build a hut, or how to cook food.

A rescue message How would you get a message to a passing aeroplane or ship? What would you write or draw? (Remember that people might not understand English.)

An explorer's description Think of all the interesting plants and animals you might see. Write an account of how you travelled around the island and describe all the things you saw.

A map Draw a map showing all the rivers, mountains, forests, caves, etc. They all need to be given invented names.

Something to Sell

Advertisements are a way of telling people about things that are for sale. However, they don't always tell you everything you need to know.

 Jenny wants to sell her bike. The newsagent said she could put a postcard advertisement in the shop window for 50p per week.

Jenny had to work out what she would say in her advertisement. She began by making a list, in rough, of all the good and bad things about her bike.

GOOD	BAD
Works quite well	rusty
3 gears	too small for a 10-year-old
red 'Thunderer Special'	mudguards bent
has lights	back light broken
got it new from shop	pump missing

Then she wrote her advertisement out on a postcard like this:

FOR SALE

RED " THUNDERER SPECIAL " IN MARVELLOUS

CONDITION. 3 GEARS. FRONT AND REAR

LIGHTS .

£ 50   Jenny Kennedy
         17 High Street

Is everything in it **true**? How is the advertisement different from the lists she wrote? Why do you think it is different?

Now look at these other advertisements. They tell you the good points. But do you think there might be some **bad** points which are not mentioned?

Make a list of things that might be wrong with each of the items advertised. (You can start by saying The records might be scratched.)

Which do you think might be the worst thing to buy? Why?

Make up some postcard advertisements for things **you** might want to sell, for example:

    stamp collections
    records
    toys
    your little brother or sister

What do People Really Say?

Would this girl say

You can not catch me!

or

You can't catch me!

Would this boy say

What's for tea?

or

What is for tea?

Would this lady say

I am going for a walk

or

I'm going for a walk

Would this man say

You're not funny!

or

You are not funny!

Would this boy say

It's not fair!

or

It is not fair!

Look at the apostrophes ('). Can you explain why they are used?

Apostrophes

Put an apostrophe where you miss out letters.

When people are talking:

is not changes to **isn't**   **do not** changes to **don't**
it is changes to **it's**   **I will** changes to **I'll**
I am changes to **I'm**   **let us** changes to **let's**

 What do people say instead of these?

that is	I would not
he is	he could not
we are	you must not
you have	we should not

Can you think of any more shortened forms?

Copy out this opening for a story. Change the pink words into the shortened form using an apostrophe.

The Incredible Invention

"**What is** that horrible object **you have** got there?" said my dad.
"Oh nothing, Dad," I said. "**It is** just something **I am** inventing."
"**You are** not bringing it into this house. Get it out!" he said firmly.
"Oh Dad!" I cried. "You **will not** even notice it once **it is** in my bedroom."

Check that you have put the apostrophes in the right places, then carry on with the story. What is the incredible invention you have been making? What does it do? What does your Dad think of it?

The Winner

Read this play together. There are three characters: Alex, Lisa and Mum.

Mum Come on, get on with your breakfast. You've got to leave for school in ten minutes. Where's Alex?

Lisa Having a bath, I think.

Mum A bath at this time of the morning? That child is crazy! Alex!

Lisa He's a bit grubby, Mum. He got up early to paint his new farm model.

Mum Oh no. That is the limit. Alex! Alex! Come here at once!

(Alex appears at the door wearing only a towel.)

Mum Oh my goodness! I'll have to sit down. Alex, you have five minutes to get ready for school. You've got green and yellow paint on your arms and face and in your hair, and you're still not dressed.

Alex Sorry Mum. The paint won't come off. It's all sticky.

Mum I give up. I'll have to explain to your teacher that . . . .

Alex I said sorry Mum. Hey – the post has come.

Lisa I'll get it!

A boring looking one for you, Mum. A catalogue for Dad. And . . . Wow! This one's for me! I wonder what it is.

Alex Open it quick Lisa.

Lisa Hey! Wowee! Mum! I've won! I've won the competition!

Mum and Alex What competition Lisa? What have you won?

You carry on with the play.

Think: What sort of competition has Lisa won? What is the prize? What do they all say? Does Alex get the paint off? Does Mum manage to get them off to school?

You can start like this:

The Winner

Lisa   Mum! I've won the competition!

Mum and Alex   What competition Lisa? What have you won?

Lisa   I was keeping it a secret. Last month I . . .

Extra Idea

Write a play about breakfast time in your own family. Is there a rush? Try to include what people really say in your family. Then perhaps a very surprising letter arrives from a distant relation. Or perhaps you look out of the window and see something very unusual.

Writing a Play

Choose one of these starting points for a play.

The Fantastic New Pupil

Characters   Assad
Maria
Gary
Joel
The new pupil

Assad   Listen everybody! I've just seen the most fantastic-looking kid walking towards the school!

Maria   Mrs Britton said a new child was joining our class today. What's so fantastic about him?

You can change the teacher's and children's names to those in your own class if you like. What happens when the new pupil walks in? Is it a boy or a girl?

What is fantastic about the child?

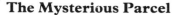

The Mysterious Parcel

Characters   Rumple
Dad
———
———

Dad   Wake up, Rumple! Happy birthday!

Rumple   Urrrh! What? My birthday? Wow! Are there any presents?

Dad   Not this year, I'm afraid. We've run out of money.

Rumple   What? No presents?

Dad   I was joking. Look, this huge parcel was delivered yesterday by a strange-looking man.

You can change Rumple's name if you want to. What mysterious thing is in the parcel? What happens? You can invent some extra characters.

The Rescue

Characters   Lord Quentin
Jan Clifford
Soldiers and servants
Robin Hood
Robin's men.

Lord Quentin   I've captured you at last, Jan Clifford. Never again will you be able to steal my deer. Soldiers, take him to the dungeon!

What does Jan reply? Carry on with the play. Probably Robin Hood will make plans with his men to carry out a rescue.

Missing

Characters _____
_____
_____

_____   He should have been home ages ago. I hope nothing's happened to him.

_____   Don't worry, I expect he's all right. If he's not here by eight o'clock we'll phone the police.

Think of names for the characters. Who is missing? What happens?

or you might have another idea of your own for a play.

Serious Problems

Talk about these problems with your teacher before you start writing anything. You might also want to act them out.

Stealing

Imagine that you have seen an older child in your school going through other children's coat pockets in search of money. Think what you would do.

Would you

pretend you hadn't seen it and keep quiet? Why?

tell the child that you have seen? If so, what would you say? Why?

tell your friends? What would they say?

tell a teacher? Then what would happen?

Do you have any other ideas?

Now, **write down** what you would do. Start If I saw an older child stealing... and explain what you think would happen.

Teasing

What is happening in this picture? What do you think people are saying?

How did it start? What is the girl thinking? Why are **all** the other children joining in?

Write a story called Teasing. (Make it true to life but don't use people's real names.)

Puzzle Letters

Anthony wrote this letter to his friend Janet, using secret picture writing.

Ja ,

hope U R .

On day went 2 a and

our team dow. T went 2

have T with my friend Ti y at s

. Our was ow on 2s day.

He f in a deep and caught

a ld ne. gave m 6/+3 of my

2 make m f better.

c u soon

from

hony

Can you understand it?

Now write your own puzzle letter to a friend. These words might give you some more ideas.

and can ring

all at in

Ideas for Daft Rhymes

In all these rhymes it is important to keep the rhythm or beat.
Read them aloud several times.

1 Mike Rosen wrote these *Down Behind the Dustbin* poems. Read them and try to write some more like them.

They don't have to rhyme. Names you might use are Sue, Anne, Jack, Fred, Sam, Nancy.

Down behind the dustbin
I met a dog called Ted.
"Leave me alone," he says,
"I'm just going to bed."

Down behind the dustbin
I met a dog called Felicity.
"It's a bit dark here," she said,
"They've cut off the electricity."

Down behind the dustbin
I met a dog called Roger.
"Do you own this bin?" I said.
"No. I'm only the lodger."

Down behind the dustbin
I met a dog called Billy.
"I'm not talking to you," I said,
"if you're going to be silly."

Down behind the dustbin
I met a dog called Barry.
He tried to take the bin away
but it was too heavy to carry.

Down behind the dustbin
I met a dog called Mary.
"I wish I wasn't a dog," she said.
"I wish I was a canary.'

2 This rhyme is chanted by American children as they walk along a pavement trying not to step on the lines.

Step on a Crack

Step on a crack,
You'll break your mother's back;
Step on a line,
You'll break your father's spine.

Step in a ditch,
Your mother's nose will itch;
Step in the dirt,
You'll tear your father's shirt.

Write some more verses for this rhyme starting:

Step on a cat
You'll _____
Step on a _____
You'll _____

58

More Characters for You to Write About

Here are some characters from famous books. They might give you ideas for writing, but of course you can alter the names.

Mary Poppins, the magic nanny.

Charlie Cornett is always trying out new ideas and getting into trouble.

Polly and Digory on their flying horse.

Mowgli, the jungle boy and friend to all animals.

Margaret Thursday, the orphan who knows how to look after herself.

Specs McCann who looks a snob but has magic gifts.

Index of Skills and Types of Writing

Page numbers in bold type indicate that a skill is the main objective of that unit. Page numbers in light type indicate that a skill is touched on in that unit or is included in Extra Ideas.